Inauguration Day

The White House

The Grand Ball

Air Force One

The Vice President, Mike Pence

President Trump and The First Lady Melania

The Presidential Farewell

At the White House balcony

The President's First Address to Congress

Memorial Day at Arlington National Cemetery

The Rose Garden

Vice President Mike Pence in the Blue Room

President Trump at the Wailing Wall in Israel

First Lady Melania at the Wailing Wall in Israel

Remembrance Wreath Laying

Vice President Mike Pence, President Donald J. Trump and Speaker of the House, Paul Ryan, during the President's

First Address to Congress

Entering the Rotunda of the U.S. Capitol Building

Aboard Ari Force One on the Phone

Holding Hands at the Vatican

Hugs

Waving to the crowd

Craft day with the First Lady

Greetings from the President

Saying Good-Bye